American Jaguar
A Book of Poems
by Cathy Brichoux

Table of Contents:

5. Pink with Black and Brown

7. Graduation Day!

9. Wishing For a Friend

13. Deceptive Love

15. This Part of Me Is Missing

17. Pregnant

21. Her Birthday Prayer

23. A Tale of Two Siblings

29. Cher VII

35. Crated Cat

37. Ode to Earth

39. Ode to Old Sol

41. Ode to Luna

45. Sixth Grade Blessings

47. Sensible Friend

51. Little Piggy Percentages

55. Covered Wagons

57. Jaguar

Pink with Black and Brown

                    dog handle swings high
                      Black and Brown
                      blur south   flowers
                      trotting north   lawn cement
                      to his hand   blacktop divide
                      kind pats   white metal boxes
                      encouraged   west white metal
                      swings around   doors open
                      loads dog handle
                      high above
                      swings
                      south
                      Black
                      blurs
                       Brown
                        sniffs
                        green
                        north
                        Black
                         blurs
                         south
                          Pink's
                          hands
                          open
                          wide
                          grab
                          ball
                          pats
                          Black
                         Pink's
                         voice
                        Brown
                        sniffs
                       green
                       ground
                       Black
                       sniffs
                      green
                      ground
                   Pink
                 sniffs
              blue
            air

6

Graduation Day!

Put down all your work and come watch me walk.
For so many years, to you, today was just talk.
Listen! The ringing of voices all through the hall.
To me that stage looks large. To you it's small.

Sit and listen deep to the words in each speech.
Resounding wisdom to our souls will reach.
Next each name is mentioned with pride loudly pronounced;
We clap for each graduate as they are announced.

Two years, four, six, eight or more of our best.
We stand and receive reward for our quests.
So proud I will turn and look toward you.
In that moment feel uplifted starting all new.

You've been there for me Mom, Dad, family and friends
through good and bad times…life's long twisty bends.
Far in the distance you clap, while I smile.
Our future is bright since you're with me the whole while.

Wishing for a Friend

I wish I had a friend like me.
I know just what I'd get.
On every topic, we'd agree.
I haven't found her yet.

We'd play with birds and crochet too.
Our conversation would just rock.
No more cleaning houses solo,
Cells glued to ear; we'd talk.

Heavy objects, in place would stay.
I'd never get much rest.
And she'd need naps too much, I'd say,
too much for a clean nest.

So, some things might not ever get done.
Some things would go un-said.
My masterpiece relationship,
just fell apart inside my head.

I guess she wouldn't be the one
to keep my friendship fed,
because I have just this much fun,
and half of what needs said.

I guess I need someone who's strong
and not a bit like me.
Someone who sings their diverse song,
but my points, they can see.

Someone to get along with, rare,
that knows how not to fight.
About their background, I won't care!
I think I see the light!

We don't have to be the same at all
to get along together.
So, she or he could be real tall,
could be scared of nasty weather.

They might not crochet or love to talk,
or know about animals,
but they could like to go for a walk
and listen to my tall tales.

They'd learn about all that I know.
I'd learn from them as well.
Our friendship would be really slow.
They're secrets, I'd never tell!

Loyalty, I guess is a must
and honesty as well,
forgiveness and a lot of trust.
Humor makes for a smooth sail!

But in the end two people lead,
walking close, side by side.
Opposites attract, I've read.
That kind of love can't hide.

I might as well stop my searching
and appreciate who's here.
Stop trying to perfect, perfecting.
The clouds part. All is clear!

Here my friends were, all around me!
Every day of ever year!
I'll be the best friend I can be
to all those who draw near.

Cause they're the ones I'm asking for,
the ones I crave to see.
They're looking all around themselves
and they're asking God, for me.

12

Deceptive Love

Love is red.
Hate is blue.
I'd rather have a friend that's true.

Betray, try, try,
then say good-bye.
When games are played it goes awry.

How we treat,
how we greet,
makes a difference in who we meet.

Friends forever,
seen hardly ever,
are better than betrayal that's clever.

14

This Part of Me Is Missing

This part of me is missing.
This part of me is dead.

Along with my first kissing,
a memory deep inside my head.

I wind up here when I get scared
and life's way too hard to bare.

The oddest moments I have shared.
Deep pain drives me right back here.

Memories made with loved ones
and all the times I went the max.

Those will help old crippled bones.
In my sweet memories, I'll relax.

16

Pregnant

I thought I was sick
I thought I was lazy
But as it turns out
I was making a baby.

Walking side to side and singing her favorite song,
she wiggle waggles, as she waddles along.

Craving bacon and strawberries, planning each and every meal,
aromas bring strong passion, as it's now a real big deal.

Some things are more important, then they ever were before.
To the baby inside her, allegiance she's already swore.

Buying more clothes, shoes and jewelry, then she did all last year.
What she doesn't outgrow, she wears out faster, it's clear.

Getting ready for a baby, there's just lots to get done.
While expecting her daughter, she's caring for her son.

The yard's ready, waiting for those little, tiny feet.
Hers are a half size larger, their growth still not complete.

She's widening her pathways and watching side to side.
Her parts are bigger, better, she bumps into things at times.

A bedroom wall to build, painting, carpet to install.
Baby's room is forming, planned for one real small.

Her world is expanding, still learning how to paint
fairy prints and forest landscape, without complaint.

Knitting, crochet, sewing, all come back to her mind.
After seascapes and penguins, her talents combine.

Because it's unexpected, she didn't have to wait.
Miracles are wonderful! God's mercy isn't late.

Getting the job done and learning new songs,
she's become a bigger person, forgiven past wrongs.

Her heart and soul are bigger, and they continue to grow.
After baby comes expect more growth of heart and soul.

Cheerful, relaxed, happy, that's the goal of her day.
Rest enough, eat right and remember to pray.

Each day is a miracle wrapped in mercy and grace.
Progression, not perfection and jumping into the race.

Pay it forward big time is the order of the day.
Selfless concept and reflection, as she continues to pay.

And wiggle waggle waddles along.
She wiggle waggle waddles along.

19

20

Her Birthday Prayer

With her kittens tucked in
my three-year old said,
"Good night" to the Moon
and off I was led.

"You'll be four in the morning.
What do you pray for?"
"Dear Lord, I want honey,
beach balls and keys.
keys for all the key holes,
and more beach balls please."

With her, "Thank you Lord,"
I kissed her forehead,
lifted her covers and to her
many books I read.

A Tale of Two Siblings

I'm not sure where to start this.
The middle seems just right.
So, here I go, my tale to tell.
I hope it brings some light.

I have a little sister.
She's two and really cute.
Her hair's so long and brown.
Her eyes are big and bright blue.

She likes princesses, dogs, cats, and birds,
to dress herself, play with baby dolls and brooms.
If she's sad I try to cheer her up,
tickle, dance, whatever it takes.

I make her laugh and smile again,
cause I like her and that's a fact.
Sometimes she can be Rug Rat-ish
and that's okay, cause now I'm not so Bratt-ish

She climbs all over the furniture.
She jumps around the floor.
She does some things I used to do,
things I don't do anymore.

She's like a little mirror to me.
I can see myself so clearly.
She doesn't do all that I did,
hasn't had time to act so severely.

I used to pick my nose,
hit, kick, spit and more.
I threw things across the room,
painted our living room pink.

I used to be cruel and mean.
I loved to hurt and break things.
I threw anything next to me
just for fun, just to see it fly and land.

I didn't care who I would hurt.
I yelled "I hate you!" many times.
I didn't understand, you see,
how others felt up next to me.

The hate I felt warmed up my heart.
The callousness felt good.
They stuck around and took it all, especially my parents.
I couldn't figure out just why two people would do that.

But, now I know. Their hearts gave them no choice.
I am their son and their love has won.
God must have had a hand in.
I'm eternally grateful for that.

My parents gave me everything.
I asked and, "Bam!" it appeared.
Completely spoiled and pampered,
I only learned to take, that's now real clear.

I lied and hurt myself so much
trying to prove I wasn't loved
to strangers all around me.
I reached out, then punished them too, for their love.

I admit Sis doesn't do half the things
that I am known to do.
But, I stopped all short, immediately.
With all that stuff, I'm through!

I saw her pick her nose, you see
and that was all it took!
I'd picked my nose that very day!
It was like the earth just shook!!!

I used to roll on furniture,
until I saw her do it.
"She could of killed herself!" I thought.
My heart felt like a dagger went through it!

It's no longer just a joke.
"No more!" I said to my own self.
This is it! End of the line!
Today I start being a good brother!

I think she needs someone real strong,
someone who'll protect and comfort her.
Someone to joke around with,
but, safely, that's for sure!

She needs to know how to get along
with the other kids around her.
So, that's my goal, from this day forth,
I'll make sure friends and family surround her.

Because I'd never really loved before,
I didn't understand it.
When sis came to our home something changed
inside me, like maybe God had planned it.

At times she seemed so threatening.
At times I was grateful she was here.
With sister home my parents couldn't give
one hundred percent only to me.

I had to learn to share and now
I even know how to give.
I learned to love myself and then
I learned to love my parents.

It wasn't a stretch to spread that love
to shape and grow and share it.
First, I liked my sister.
And now I even like other kids.

I used to think I understood.
I thought I really knew.
I thought I already liked everyone,
no matter who.

Now I know the difference between family and friends.
I know that strangers are not friends,
that sisters are separate too.
In teaching her, I learned personal space.

After 10 years of others failing,
she taught me without trying at all.
I taught myself, so I could teach her.
That was my key to learning.

We'll be a team, my sis and me.
We'll help others and I'm sure
I'll be a vet, firefighter, more.
She'll dance, she'll sing and teach.

Someday we'll be a big family.
Her kids and mine will play.
Our spouses will be BFF's.
That's just the way it will stay.

Now I have a future, a family and friends.
I don't spit in God's eye anymore!
I look up at him and I say,
"Thank you, God! Just Thank you!"

That's all I've got to say.

28

Cher VII

I

Deep within the heart of Woman,
decide: fear, impulsive disgust,
or Love, Understanding and Acceptance,
along with Cautious Trust.

On cluttered counter, you appear.
I grab glasses, for close inspection.
For child of seven generations,
my self-control means your salvation.

Cheiracanthium mildei, my friend.
Past names will never do.
Seven forms, Anne, Thia, Raca,
Muith, Nacar, Ant and now Cher.

Yellow sac so new,
young tan skinny legs stretch.
Sternum, a different pattern,
this year only brownish green.

II

The next encounter larger, faster.
Yet, familiarity breeds brave moves.
You're not a cat, so don't go there!
Shoulders, legs, off limits Cher!

Sprint to pink towel across the counter.
Wait like a squirrel crossing a road.
Shared glances, mutual inspections,
swinging freely from your silk.

For your safety I'm jumping back now.
About my business, still I go.
But watch your acrobatics,
cabinet to wall, fast, then slow.

Sucking something, labium fastened,
love the wall, all unwashed.
Setting palpi, silk to silk, up and
up and southward, behind the toilet.

Directly, on the red silk rose,
set on back of the white toilet,
you pose for just one photo
on, what I now know, is *your* rose.

Laughter fills the room.
You crawl, zig zag along the wall.
Your bed is waiting up in a corner.
Bated breath lest you should fall.

The white silk here, there,
this wall, this ceiling,
this corner and everywhere
obvious, yet previously ignored.

Respectful notions of clean sinks,
bill bugs, weevils, beetles,
noted now, have not been seen.
Short lived relief, all is temporary.

Welcome Cher, until summer.
Then, into our garden you will go.
If you want to, no hurry sweet thing.
In houseplants, no doubt, you'll show.

III

There, you've found it!
Your bed of white silk,
so round and fluffy,
undisturbed, inviting, warm!

Inspection, here there,
all around and moving faster,
check the bug wrapped neatly nearby.
Dotting this way and that way.

Zipping backward,
then you move forward,
into your silk bed,
a round, previously empty hole.

We're both relaxed now.
Night-time is for hunting.
All the day, you'll sleep.
This I know, nocturnal Cher.

Sweet Arachnid dreams
of grabbing bill bugs,
warehouse beetles,
broad-nosed weevils.

Summer signs are everywhere!
New leaves, fresh flowers,
and Cher... snug day sleeper,
up in her corner, without a care!

34

Crated Cat

I'm loved, why don't I feel it?
Empty inside, just hollow space.
The others seem to know
I'm here, in this tiny place.

Felt it before the cold time.
I can't reach back past their stealing.
Safe, you worked, with me inside my crate.
Your shirt, my toys, food, litter & water.

Sudden noises, heavy footsteps.
I was sick from motion.
I arrived here, smells foreign.
The air forever now is cold.

They pull me out, like a doll off a shelf.
I feel lost, new toys, new smells.
Hiss, scratch, hide, they lose interest.
I'm back in my crate with your smell fading.

They leave at night and it's dark in here.
The lights are all out and dogs lay as they fell.
You're not here, so I'm confused.
I'm touched with fear and I don't feel well.

I'm curled up, imagining you to sleep.
In dreams we're together, life's not bizarre.
Awakening is torturous, like a nightmare!
I'm wondering why I am and where you are.

36

Ode to Earth

Payette River, winding, driven, strong, exciting.
Ridge of pines so dense, green, mixed with sky.
Mountains lifting spirits high above the crowds below.
Quiet energy strengthens my bones.

Without you, I cannot live, cannot live at all!
Your mountains calm my nerves, comfort my broken heart.
Your rivers heal all my wounds, pick me up, set me on course.
Your trees and flowers hold me with loving pine scented air.

Mother, your boulders prop me up and cradle me.
Your messengers: Blue Bird, Raven, Sparrow,
Squirrel, Deer, Rabbit, Bear, Cougar,
precious in my heart, that beats only for you.

Within your majesty, I find peace.
Within your scenery, I find grace.

Ode to Old Sol

Sol, my friend, my enemy.
With you, energy abounds.
93,000,000 miles away, you rule my life.
8 minutes just to shine on me,
Yellow, blue, white, green and red, rainbows you create.
One hour with you and my energy fills, gravity loosens her grip.
Clouds compete with my eyes.
Your rays I crave, your rays I chase, your rays I make time for.
One hour daily is yours. all yours and yet, that hour can't be fixed.
You come and go, hide, peek and shine when you do
and not for me. You don't know me.
I see you. You don't see me.
I'm down here dying, crying, sleeping, looking out for you.
So, I love you, hate you, need you, and don't want you.
I wish I could be free!

40

Ode to Luna

Luna waxing, waning,
circling our mother, Earth,
you phase in and out.

Waxed nights I see your
grey maps on canvas white
patterned inside your circle,
charging my empath crystals.
I've seen you with red rings,
golden, glowing due to weather.

Folk stories say you rule tides,
women's moods, and wolf song.
As natural guide surrounded by stars
Earth's first child, my big sister.

Beyond Sol's whorish clouds
illuminated 238,900 miles away
a billion years younger than his 4.6,
your rare appearance always
a sweet surprise and my comfort.

Black Tourmaline, Hematite,
Labradorite, Amethyst
charged by your glow.
You protect me all day,
though I might not see you.

In rainbow-like splendor
you change hue to yellow,
blue, pink, orange and
blood moon magnificence.

My goal is to notice you more,
spend more time in your glow,
be charged by your energy,
get to know my big sister,
and notice your absence,
your blue moon phases.

44

Sixth Grade Blessings

Yellow flowered blanket surrounds her
at her curved art desk.
Ignoring her mouse,
she scrolls through lesson 8.

Huddled, heads together,
math problems need solved.
I'm teaching her mechanics
for life's future puzzles.

Comfort hugs are lengthy.
Rare giggles inspired by mistakes.
Life's easier with laughter.
The week went so quick.

46

Sensible Friendship

I

It's not my job to paint your sky blue,
bring you rainbows or cause pink sunsets.
It's not my job to make your rain land safe
in your barrel, send it back to clouds,
swollen creek beds, rivers into oceans.
But, if you need umbrella kindness,
when you can't see with your healthy eyes,
I'm always here to point things out chum
or just to help you to visualize.

II

It's not my job to judge your morals,
step inside your pure or wicked skin.
It's not my job to be your braveness,
run from crimes, critique your wrongs from rights,
preventing disasters, deciding.
But if you need some heartfelt goodness,
and can't tell others those things you know,
I'm here for you, reaching out daily
to help you label what's authentic.

III

It's not my job to label your feelings.
tell you that you're hot or that you're cold.
It's not my job to rule pain from bliss,
or to say you're not capable, numb,

causing you scars outward or inward.
But if you need a knuckle bump, hug,
to share a smile, or a real good cry,
I'm always ready, willing, waiting
to give you well-earned validation.

IV

It's not my job to make your food taste
like it's heaven on your tongue's palate.
It's not my job to make things taste sweet,
sour, bitter, nutty, carbonated,
oily, smooth, crunchy, or just plain bland.

But if you're not appreciating
I'm here to lift your spirits, and
I'll remind you life's your own banquet,
so reach out and work toward your best.

V

It's not my job to clear your air, relieve
your conscience or keep dust from stirring.
It's not my job to keep your atmosphere
crystal clean, with no fog or fire's smoke,
like a dome protecting everything.
But, if you need a clue or filter
for your breath or to clear perception,
I'm here to bounce ideas off your chest,
help examine issues on your own.

VI

It's not my job to lie, tickle your ears
with white noise, frequencies to control.
It's not my job to hide the truth from you,
whisper sweet nothings, temporary
bombs waiting to go off in your space.
But, if you need a witness, I'm here,
backing you up, doing you solids.
I'm here to witness truth, help you find
yours, not necessarily my own.

50

Little Piggy Percentages

All or nothing, one hundred percent,
shopping, movies, work, play,
a strong shoulder for lent,
always there for each other, hey!

Some people expect one hundred percent.
It's like some want all or nothing.
But most can do only a hint
of what others still need doing.

One friend goes to market.
One friend just stays home.
One friend eats roast beef for dinner.
One friend just has none.

The concept of friends in pieces,
of friends being 80 percent.
one friend for help writing a thesis,
one for shopping or for help with the rent.

One friend can lend an ear, say?
But not a penny can they spend.
While one can shop all day,
give you presents no end.

One friend can maybe shop and talk,
while another can do neither.
Still they both are loved and walk
part of our pack or maybe a leader.

The concept that we all are pieces
of some greater puzzle, then ourselves,
sends some saying wee wee wees
all the way home by themselves.

The fact that some have more to give
and some need more to take
leaves some heads like a sieve,
while others think, "Piece of cake!"

If we all sized each other up,
then accepted what we each saw,
loved each other's measuring cup
and just asked, "What's up?"

Unusual people together would be commonplace.
Diverse groups could work together and play.
Earth could accomplish conquering space.
There's no limit, no percentage, no tether.

One has only five percent to give.
Their differences are many.
One can handle ninety and live.
Things come easy to them, like candy.

The thing is we are born with the right
to be here on this earth God lent.
Friendships shouldn't end in a fight,
because one expects one hundred percent.

To expect such a huge universal dent
is just too much for one guy to bare.
Anything more than our own small percent
could be considered criminally unfair.

So look at that person sitting next to you.
Now see them real clearly, you can.
They can't do it all, but neither can you.
Stop expecting and you'll understand.

Happiness doesn't come from doing it all.
Each brings his own percent to the table.
Let's appreciate others, ourselves great and small,
stop expecting what's best left to fable.

If the Big Toe Piggy could run all the way home,
or if Wee Wee ate all the roast beef,
would the Market Pig be worth less than some,
'cause he wasn't home and he didn't eat beef?

Covered Wagons

It wasn't long before the clouds poured rain.
Winter left and in came spring.
Life on the prairie began to thrive again.
Some mushrooms formed a fairy ring.

Her dress was patched, put together with love
The dirt, walking on and on, then stopping to rest.
Tired as they were, the children still could chase a dove.
Dinner was dandelion stew and apples at best.

Faith filled their hearts as they lay down to sleep.
Beliefs from long ago, rock solid and strong.
Everyone prayed the same prayer, their soul to keep.
Insomnia didn't exist, they woke to Cook's gong.

Sunshine, blue sky, clear with few billowy clouds.
From the east, as the sun, they came and moved west,
walked on in growing, ever increasing, crowds,
Natives not yet seeing them as their pests.

The east came west, and the far east filled emptied space.
Wars emptied lands, people multiplied, duplicated.
Today migrants spread, we push against the human race.
The cycle rises again, just as it was always fated.

56

Jaguar

My ancient rhythms, deep inside, the jungle where I roam.
Leaves brush me as I pass, panther pacing, paws plod man's path.
Air filled with stories read through nostrils lifted high.
Millions of years of imprinted instinct guide me through each line.

My musk mixes with jasmine, ginger, overpowers the orchid.
White claws scratch my sign on the surface of the soft ground,
warning other jaguars to stay clear today.
My warm pool freshly filled from rain, awaits me.

Cooling my muscles, refreshing my weary body,
rosettes submerge, fur engulfed for cleaning and relaxation.
Resting my full belly deep beneath my powerful spine
my head rests on my forepaws. I close my golden eyes.

Memories of the hunt, caiman thrashing side to side,
my jaws gripped tightly round and behind my caiman's neck.
Crunching powerful jaws disconnect electric flow.
My ancestors ate their ancestor's gator tender loins.

I remember times behind me, mates and kits long gone,
a mother's kindness, educating me in the ancient ways.
I remember resting watching man crossing along his paths.
Laughter fills my memories, native chatter, music and dance.

Reminiscing satisfied with life's past and present.
Warmth of daylight reaches my pool, warms my body.
Relaxed, I nap and dream of meeting my mate.
Years of kit mischief, educating, watching my young jaguars play.

I live a whole lifetime, surrounded by vivid colors, smells and sounds.
As my eyes crack open, it's beetles that first greet me.
Then, Squirrel tumbles breakfast, Boat Billed Heron perched nearby.
Howler Monkey yodels as Red Deer's yummy scent whiffing, mixes.

Up, up, dripping wet, I shake heavily soaked unique rosetted fur.
I'm padding south toward next night's hunting grounds.
Summer's heat overtakes me, slowly padding I pace man's road.
To a high spot, watching post, man and beast I rule from above.

Through the day, with tail swishing, I'm thoughtful in my way.
Man's dogs bark a warning unheeded. Table scraps close their mouths.
I watch and sometimes nap, my presence hidden safe from man.
Four million years of tradition is tucked in my brave warm heart.

59

www.ingramcontent.com/pod-product-compliance
Lightning Source LLC
Chambersburg PA
CBHW032007220426
43664CB00005B/170